Foliage

Leaves and Needles to Color

Grayscale Adult Coloring Book

A Galleria Monte Art Project

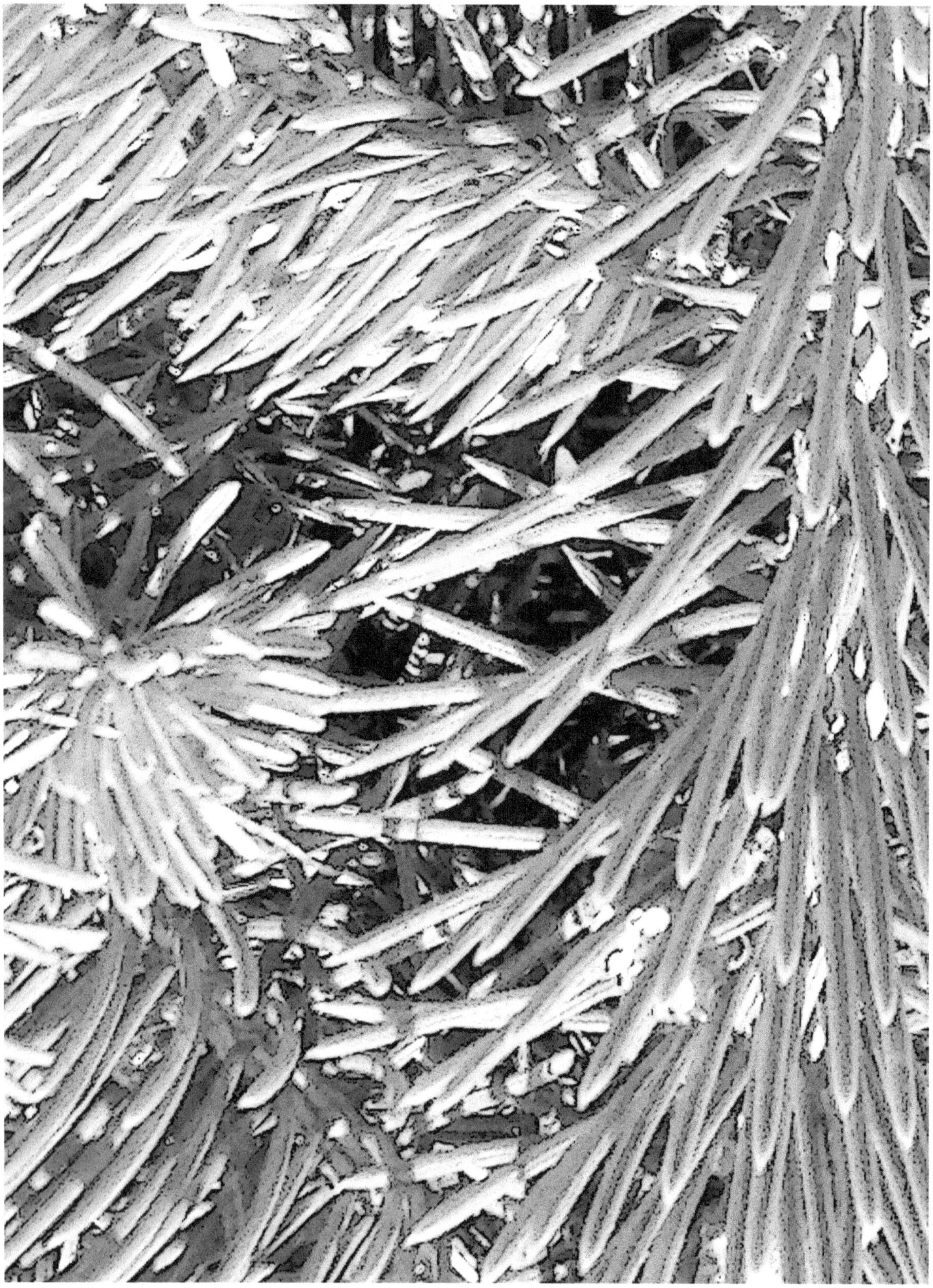

www.ingramcontent.com/pod-product-compliance
Lightning Source LLC
Chambersburg PA
CBHW081116280526
45787CB00007B/2854
9781534990180